Digital Marketing

First Steps

Creating a successful digital marketing campaign involves careful planning, strategy development, and execution.

Overview

Creating a successful digital marketing campaign involves careful planning, strategy development, and execution. Here are the first steps you should consider when starting a digital marketing campaign:

1. **Identify your industry and benchmarks:**
   Determine which industry your business or campaign belongs to and then identify your key industry standards. This step is crucial for understanding your position in the market, setting realistic goals, and measuring the success of your digital marketing campaign.

2. **Define Your Goals and Objectives:**
   Determine what you want to achieve with your campaign. Are you looking to increase brand awareness, drive website traffic, generate leads, boost sales, or something else? Your goals will guide your entire campaign strategy.

3. **Know Your Target Audience:**
   Identify your target audience's demographics, interests, behaviors, and pain points. Understanding your audience will help you create content and choose the right platforms to reach them effectively.

4. **Choose Your Digital Marketing Channels:**
   Based on your target audience and campaign goals, select the most suitable digital marketing channels. These could include social media (Facebook, Instagram, Twitter, LinkedIn), display network, Connected TV, Digital Out of Home, email marketing, content marketing, influencer marketing, and more.

5. **Develop a Budget:**
Determine how much you're willing to invest in your campaign. Your budget will impact your strategies, channels, and the scale of your campaign.

6. **Create a Campaign Strategy:**
Outline the overall strategy for your campaign, including messaging, content types (videos, blog posts, infographics, etc.), frequency of posts, and the timeline. Your strategy should align with your goals and target audience.

7. **Content Creation:**
Develop compelling and relevant content that resonates with your audience. Ensure that your content is engaging, valuable, and tailored to the specific platform you're using.

8. **Set Up Tracking and Analytics:**
Implement tracking tools like Google Analytics, Facebook Pixel, or other relevant tracking codes to measure the performance of your campaign. This will help you understand which strategies are working and where adjustments are needed.

9. **Create a Landing Page or Campaign Website:**
If your campaign requires driving traffic to a specific offer or product, create a dedicated landing page or website that is optimized for conversions. This page should have clear calls-to-action and relevant information.

10. **Design Visual Assets:**
Create eye-catching visuals that are consistent with your brand identity. Visual content such as images, videos, and graphics can greatly enhance the effectiveness of your campaign.

11. Schedule and Execute:

Plan out the timing of your campaign's content distribution across different channels. Use social media scheduling tools to maintain a consistent posting schedule.

12. Monitor and Optimize:

Regularly monitor the performance of your campaign using analytics. Track metrics like engagement, clicks, conversions, and ROI. Use the data to optimize your strategies and make necessary adjustments to improve results.

13. Engage and Respond:

Engage with your audience by responding to comments, messages, and feedback promptly. Building a rapport with your audience can enhance the overall success of your campaign.

14. Evaluate and Learn:

Once your campaign concludes, evaluate the results against your initial goals. Identify what worked well and what didn't. Use these insights to improve your future campaigns.

Remember, successful digital marketing campaigns require continuous learning and adaptation. Stay up-to-date with industry trends, be open to trying new strategies, and refine your approach based on the feedback and data you receive.

Identify your industry and benchmarks

Identifying the right industry for your display advertising campaign involves understanding your business's products or services, target audience, and the broader market landscape. Here's how you can go about it:

1. **Define Your Products or Services:**
   Clearly define what products or services your business offers. Consider their features, benefits, and unique selling points. This will help you categorize your offerings and determine the industry they belong to.

2. **Research Similar Businesses:**
   Look for businesses that offer similar products or services. Analyze how they position themselves, the industry they consider themselves a part of, and the type of advertising they use. This can give you insights into how your offerings fit within a specific industry.

3. **Audience Analysis:**
   Understand your target audience's demographics, interests, and behaviors. The industry you choose should align with the interests and needs of your audience. For example, if you're selling fitness equipment, you might belong to the health and wellness industry.

4. **Competitor Analysis:**
   Research your competitors and analyze the industry categories they use in their advertising. This can provide insights into the industry norms and expectations in your market.

5. **Market Trends:**

   Stay updated with industry trends and changes. Industries can evolve over time, and your products or services might fit better into a different industry due to shifts in consumer preferences or market dynamics.

6. **Keyword Research:**

   Conduct keyword research related to your offerings. Look at the keywords people use when searching for products or services similar to yours. This can give you clues about the industries those keywords are associated with.

7. **Customer Feedback:**

   Listen to customer feedback and inquiries. The questions and feedback you receive can provide valuable insights into how customers perceive your offerings and the industry context they associate with them.

8. **Consult Industry Databases:**

   Some industry databases or directories can help you find appropriate categories for your business. These databases often have predefined categories that businesses can choose from.

9. **Consider Multiple Perspectives:**

   Sometimes, a business might belong to multiple industries simultaneously. For instance, a company that offers eco-friendly cleaning products might fit into both the cleaning industry and the sustainability industry.

10. **Stay Flexible:**

    Industries can be fluid, and the category you choose might evolve as your business grows. Be open to reevaluating your industry classification as your products, services, and market landscape change.

Once you've identified the industry that best aligns with your business, you can tailor your display advertising messages, imagery, and targeting strategies to resonate with that industry's audience. Display advertising allows you to showcase your offerings to a specific audience on various websites and platforms, so selecting the right industry context is crucial for effectively reaching potential customers.

Define your Goals and Objectives

Defining clear goals and objectives is a foundational step in creating a successful digital marketing campaign. Your goals and objectives provide direction, purpose, and a measurable framework for your campaign efforts. Here's a more detailed explanation of how to define your goals and objectives:

1. **Distinguish Between Goals and Objectives:**
   Goals are the broader, qualitative aspirations you have for your campaign. They outline the desired outcome without specifying exact measurements. Objectives, on the other hand, are specific, measurable, achievable, relevant, and time-bound (SMART) targets that support your goals.

2. **Understand Different Types of Goals:**
   Depending on your business and campaign focus, goals might include:
   - Awareness: Increasing brand recognition and reaching a broader audience.
   - Engagement: Encouraging interaction, likes, shares, comments, etc.
   - Traffic: Driving more visitors to your website or landing pages.
   - Leads: Collecting contact information from potential customers.
   - Sales: Converting leads into paying customers.
   - Retention: Encouraging repeat purchases and customer loyalty.

3. **Use the SMART Criteria for Objectives:**
   SMART objectives are Specific, Measurable, Achievable, Relevant, and Time-bound. Each objective should be clear, quantifiable, feasible, aligned with your goals, and have a defined timeframe for achievement.

4. **Specificity is Key:**
   Your objectives should be precise. Instead of saying "increase website traffic," specify "increase monthly website traffic by 25% over the next three months."

5. **Measurable Metrics:**
   Define metrics that you'll use to track progress and success. For example, if your goal is lead generation, your objective might be to "generate 100 new leads per month."

6. **Achievability and Realism:**
   Set objectives that are attainable based on your resources, budget, and current business status. Setting unattainable goals can lead to frustration and inefficiency.

7. **Relevance to Business Goals:**
   Ensure that your objectives align with your overall business goals. Every objective should contribute directly to the success of your business.

8. **Time-Bound Targets:**
   Set a specific timeframe for achieving each objective. This adds urgency and helps you track progress effectively.

9. **Hierarchy of Goals and Objectives:**
   Consider the hierarchy of your goals and objectives. Objectives should support your overarching goals, and multiple objectives can contribute to a single goal.

10. Prioritize Based on Importance:

Some objectives may have a higher priority than others, depending on your business needs. Make sure your resources are allocated according to these priorities.

11. Regular Review and Adjustment:

Continuously monitor your objectives' progress and adjust them as needed. Digital marketing is dynamic, and you may need to adapt based on changing circumstances.

Example:

Goal: Increase Online Sales for a New Product Line

Objectives:

1. **Objective**: Drive Targeted Traffic to the Product Pages
   - → Specific: Increase the number of visitors to the new product pages.
   - → Measurable: Drive a minimum of 5,000 clicks to the product pages within the next two months.
   - → Achievable: Based on historical data, the campaign has the potential to achieve this level of traffic.
   - → Relevant: Directly contributes to the goal of increasing online sales for the new product line.
   - → Time-bound: Achieve this within the next two months.

2. **Objective:** Improve Click-Through Rate (CTR) on Display Ads
   - → Specific: Enhance the engagement and appeal of display ads.
   - → Measurable: Increase the average CTR from 0.5% to 1.5% by the end of the quarter.

→ <u>Achievable</u>: By creating more compelling ad creatives and targeting relevant audiences.

→ <u>Relevant</u>: Higher CTR indicates more interest and potential conversions.

→ <u>Time-bound</u>: Achieve this by the end of the quarter.

3. **Objective:** Increase Conversion Rate on Product Pages

→ <u>Specific</u>: Improve the rate at which visitors on the product pages make a purchase.

→ <u>Measurable</u>: Increase the conversion rate from 2% to 4% within the next three months.

→ <u>Achievable</u>: By optimizing the product pages, streamlining the checkout process, and using retargeting.

→ <u>Relevant</u>: Higher conversion rates directly contribute to increased online sales.

→ <u>Time-bound</u>: Achieve this within the next three months.

4. **Objective:** Retarget Abandoned Cart Users

→ <u>Specific</u>: Re-engage users who have added products to their carts but did not complete the purchase.

→ <u>Measurable</u>: Recover 15% of abandoned carts by sending targeted retargeting ads within the next month.

→ <u>Achievable</u>: Based on industry benchmarks and the effectiveness of retargeting strategies.

→ <u>Relevant</u>: Increases the likelihood of converting users who have shown interest.

→ <u>Time-bound</u>: Achieve this within the next month.

5. **Objective: Expand Brand Reach and Awareness**

→ <u>Specific</u>: Increase brand exposure and recognition for the new product line.

- → <u>Measurable</u>: Achieve a minimum of 500,000 ad impressions across relevant websites within the next quarter.
- → <u>Achievable</u>: By using a combination of display ad placements and targeting options.
- → <u>Relevant</u>: Brand awareness sets the foundation for future sales.
- → <u>Time-bound</u>: Achieve this within the next quarter.

By setting these objectives, you're creating a focused and measurable approach to your display network campaign. Each objective contributes to the overarching goal of increasing online sales for the new product line. As you implement and monitor your campaign, you can track progress toward these objectives and make necessary adjustments to optimize performance.

Know Your Target Audience

"Know Your Target Audience" is a critical aspect of any successful display advertising campaign. Understanding your audience helps you tailor your messaging, creative assets, and targeting strategies to effectively reach the right people.

1. **Demographics:**
   Understand the basic characteristics of your audience, such as age, gender, income level, education, and marital status. For instance, if you're promoting luxury watches, your target audience might be affluent individuals aged 30-50 with a higher income level.

2. **Geographic Location:**
   Determine the geographic areas where your audience is located. This could be a specific city, region, country, or even international markets. If you're a local bakery, your display ads might focus on reaching people within a certain radius of your storefront.

3. **Interests and Hobbies:**
   Identify the hobbies, interests, and activities that your audience engages in. For instance, if you're selling outdoor camping gear, your target audience might include adventure enthusiasts, hikers, and nature lovers.

4. **Behavioral Insights:**
   Analyze the online behaviors of your audience, including their browsing habits, purchase history, and engagement patterns. If you're running a fashion e-commerce store, you might target users who have previously shown interest in clothing and accessories.

5. **Psychographic Factors:**
   Dive into your audience's values, beliefs, and lifestyle choices. For example, if you're promoting eco-friendly products, your target audience might be environmentally conscious consumers.

6. **Problem Solving:**
   Understand the pain points or challenges your audience faces and how your product or service can solve them. If you're offering time management software, your ads could highlight how your solution simplifies their daily tasks.

7. **Audience Segmentation:**
   Divide your audience into segments based on shared characteristics. For instance, a travel agency might create different ads for adventure seekers, family vacationers, and honeymooners.

8. **Device and Platform Preferences:**
   Know which devices and platforms your audience prefers. This helps optimize your ads for various screen sizes and ensure they're seen where your audience spends their time. Mobile-friendly ads are crucial for capturing on-the-go users.

By understanding your target audience in depth, you can create display ads that resonate with their preferences, needs, and aspirations. This leads to higher engagement rates, better click-through rates, and ultimately, improved conversion rates for your display advertising campaign.

Examples:

Example 1: E-Commerce Apparel Store

If you're advertising a new line of athletic wear, your target audience might be:

- ➜ Demographics: Active individuals aged 18-35.
- ➜ Interests: Fitness, running, gym workouts.
- ➜ Behavioral Insights: Users who have searched for activewear brands.
- ➜ Geographic Location: Nationwide, particularly in urban areas.
- ➜ Device Preferences: Focus on mobile devices for users on the go.

Example 2: Tech Gadgets

For promoting a new smartphone model:

- ➜ Demographics: Tech-savvy individuals aged 25-40.
- ➜ Interests: Technology news, gadget reviews, mobile gaming.
- ➜ Psychographics: Early adopters, interested in cutting-edge technology.
- ➜ Geographic Location: Major cities with high-tech adoption rates.
- ➜ Device Preferences: Optimize for both mobile and desktop users.

Example 3: Home Decor

If you're advertising trendy home decor items:

- ➜ Demographics: Homeowners and renters aged 25-45.
- ➜ Interests: Interior design, home improvement, DIY projects.
- ➜ Behavioral Insights: Users who have searched for home renovation ideas.
- ➜ Geographic Location: Tailor ads to specific regions with a strong interest in home decor.

Choose Your Digital Marketing Channels

By integrating Display Network alongside social media, DOOH, and CTV at different funnel levels, you establish a comprehensive digital marketing approach that caters to objectives, audiences, and stages of the customer journey. Each channel contributes uniquely to your overall strategy, promoting brand awareness, consideration, conversions, and customer loyalty.

Upper Funnel: Prospecting and Consideration (Brand Awareness, Traffic and Consideration)

1. **Social Media:**
   → Strategy: Create engaging and shareable content to introduce your brand to a wider audience.
   → Targeting: Utilize interest-based and demographic targeting for brand exposure.
   → Example: A sustainable fashion brand can share content about its eco-friendly practices on platforms like Instagram.

2. **DOOH (Digital Out of Home):**
   → Strategy: Use DOOH to enhance brand exposure by displaying impactful visuals in high-traffic areas.
   → Targeting: Opt for general locations with high footfall.
   → Example: A tech startup can display visuals about their innovative product on digital billboards in downtown areas.

3. **Connected TV (CTV):**
   → Strategy: Deliver engaging video ads that communicate your brand story and showcase product features.

→ <u>Targeting</u>: Utilize CTV's advanced targeting options based on viewing habits.

→ <u>Example</u>: A luxury automobile brand can create CTV video ads highlighting the elegance of their latest vehicle.

4. Display Network:

→ <u>Strategy</u>: Leverage banner ads across relevant websites to expand brand visibility.

→ <u>Targeting</u>: Use demographic and interest-based targeting for broader reach.

→ <u>Example</u>: An organic skincare brand can showcase its products on lifestyle blogs frequented by health-conscious consumers.

Middle Funnel: Product Retargeting (Consideration and Intent)

1. Social Media:

→ <u>Strategy</u>: Share carousel ads showcasing products users previously viewed.

→ <u>Targeting</u>: Implement website retargeting for users who interacted with your site.

→ <u>Example</u>: An online furniture store can display carousel ads featuring products users explored.

2. Connected TV (CTV): Middle Funnel (Consideration and Evaluation)

→ <u>Strategy</u>: Deliver product demonstration videos or customer testimonials.

→ <u>Targeting</u>: Use retargeting to engage users with previous interest.

→ <u>Example</u>: An electronics retailer can showcase detailed features of a gadget through CTV video ads.

3. Display Network:

→ <u>Strategy</u>: Implement dynamic retargeting to remind users of products they viewed.

→ <u>Targeting</u>: Use website retargeting for personalized engagement.

→ <u>Example</u>: An e-commerce store can display dynamic ads showing the exact products users abandoned.

Lower Funnel: Abandoned Shopping Cart and Converters (Conversion and Loyalty)

1. Social Media:

→ <u>Strategy</u>: Deliver targeted ads featuring abandoned cart items with special offers.

→ <u>Targeting</u>: Utilize dynamic product ads for precise retargeting.

→ <u>Example</u>: A cosmetics brand can showcase skincare products in abandoned carts with limited-time discounts.

2. Display Network:

→ <u>Strategy</u>: Utilize remarketing to re-engage abandoned cart users.

→ <u>Targeting</u>: Display ads to users who left your site during the checkout process.

→ <u>Example</u>: An online bookstore can show display ads with the book titles left in abandoned carts.

Develop a Budget

Developing a budget for your digital marketing campaign is a crucial step that influences the scope, strategies, and success of your efforts. By carefully considering various factors such as reach, audience size, impressions, clicks, visits, conversions, and return on investment (ROI), you can create a budget that aligns with your campaign goals and maximizes the value of your investment.

In essence, your budget is a strategic tool that empowers you to make informed decisions about where and how to invest your resources for maximum impact. By aligning your budget with your campaign goals and closely monitoring performance, you can optimize your digital marketing efforts and achieve a strong return on investment.

Considerations When Developing Your Budget:

1. **Campaign Objectives:**
   The goals you've set for your campaign play a significant role in budget allocation. Are you aiming for brand awareness, lead generation, or direct sales? Different objectives may require varying levels of investment.

2. **Target Audience Size:**
   The size of your target audience affects how far your budget can stretch. Larger audiences may require higher investments to ensure adequate reach.

3. **Channel Selection:**
   Different digital marketing channels have varying costs associated with them. Some channels, like premium placements

on social media or high-traffic websites, might have higher costs per impression or click.

4. **Competitive Landscape:**
   Analyze your industry's competitive landscape. If your industry has high competition, you might need a more substantial budget to stand out.

5. **Geographic Reach:**
   If your campaign targets a broad geographic area, you might need to allocate more funds to cover a wider audience.

6. **Ad Format and Creatives:**
   More complex ad formats, such as video or interactive ads, may have higher production costs.

7. **Seasonality and Trends:**
   Take into account any seasonality or trends that could impact costs or demand for your products or services.

Metrics and Budget Allocation:

1. **Reach and Impressions:**
   Budget allocation can affect the number of times your ad is displayed (impressions) and the potential audience reach. Higher budgets can lead to greater exposure.

2. **Clicks and Visits:**
   More budget allocated to channels like pay-per-click (PPC) advertising can result in more clicks and visits to your website.

3. **Conversions and Cost per Action (CPA):**
    The budget's impact on conversions is critical. A higher budget can drive more conversions, leading to a lower CPA.

4. **Return on Ad Spend (ROAS):**
    ROAS reflects the revenue generated relative to your advertising expenses. A successful campaign generates revenue exceeding its costs.

Budgeting Strategies:

1. **Percentage of Revenue:**
    Allocate a fixed percentage of your projected revenue to your marketing budget. This approach can help align your budget with your business's growth.

2. **Competitor Analysis:**
    Analyze your competitors' advertising efforts and budgets to understand industry benchmarks.

3. **Test and Optimize:**
    Start with a moderate budget and gradually increase it as you gather data and optimize your campaign for better performance.

4. **Divide by Channel:**
    Allocate a portion of your budget to each chosen channel based on its potential impact on your goals.

Continuous Monitoring and Adjustment:

Regularly monitor your campaign's performance and key metrics against your budget. If a particular channel is performing exceptionally well, consider reallocating funds to capitalize on its success. Conversely, if a channel isn't delivering expected results, adjust the budget accordingly.

Create a Campaign Strategy

Creating a comprehensive campaign strategy is essential for the success of your digital marketing efforts. Your strategy serves as a roadmap that guides your messaging, content creation, posting frequency, and timeline. By aligning your strategy with your campaign goals and target audience, you can effectively engage your audience and achieve your desired outcomes.

Components of a Robust Campaign Strategy:

1. **Campaign Goals and Objectives:**
   Clearly define the specific goals and objectives of your campaign. Are you aiming to increase brand awareness, drive website traffic, generate leads, or boost sales? Each goal will inform your overall strategy.

2. **Target Audience Segmentation:**
   Segment your target audience based on demographics, behaviors, interests, and pain points. This segmentation enables you to tailor your messaging to resonate with each audience segment.

3. **Messaging and Value Proposition:**
   Craft a compelling messaging framework that highlights your brand's unique value proposition. Ensure your messaging speaks directly to the pain points and needs of your audience segments.

4. **Content Types and Formats:**

Choose the types of content that resonate with your audience and support your campaign objectives. This might include videos, blog posts, infographics, ebooks, webinars, and more.

➜ Example: For an upper funnel campaign focused on brand awareness, create engaging videos that tell your brand's story and values. For a middle funnel campaign, consider detailed blog posts that address your audience's pain points and offer solutions.

5. **Content Creation Plan:**
   Outline the content creation process, including who will be responsible for creating each type of content, the topics to be covered, and the timeline for content production.

6. **Posting Frequency and Schedule:**
   Determine how often you will publish content and engage with your audience. Consider the optimal posting frequency for each platform, ensuring a consistent presence without overwhelming your audience.

7. **Content Distribution Channels:**
   Identify the digital marketing channels you will use to distribute your content. This could include social media platforms, email marketing, Display Network, DOOH placements, and CTV advertising.

8. **Engagement and Interaction Plan:**
   Define how you will engage with your audience on each platform. Will you respond to comments, messages, and mentions promptly? How will you encourage user interaction and participation?

9. **Timeline and Milestones:**
Create a detailed timeline that outlines the start and end dates of your campaign, as well as key milestones along the way. This ensures that all team members are aligned and deadlines are met.

Example of a Campaign Strategy:

→ Campaign Objective: Increase brand awareness and drive traffic to the website.

→ Target Audience: Millennials interested in sustainable fashion.

→ Messaging: Empowering individuals to make eco-friendly fashion choices for a better planet.

→ Content Types and Formats:
- ◆ Educational blog posts about sustainable fashion practices.
- ◆ Engaging video series showcasing eco-friendly fashion brands.
- ◆ Infographics illustrating the environmental impact of fast fashion.

→ Content Creation Plan:
- ◆ Blog posts: Marketing team (weekly).
- ◆ Video series: Creative team (bi-weekly).
- ◆ Infographics: Design team (monthly).

→ Posting Frequency and Schedule:
- ◆ Blog posts: Every Tuesday and Thursday.
- ◆ Video series: Every other Friday.
- ◆ Infographics: Once a month on the 15th.

→ Content Distribution Channels:
- ◆ Social media platforms (Instagram, Facebook, Twitter).

- ◆ Display Network with a focus on fashion and sustainability websites.
- ◆ DOOH displays in eco-conscious urban areas.
- ◆ CTV advertising during eco-documentaries.
- → Engagement and Interaction Plan:
  - ◆ Respond to comments and messages within 24 hours.
  - ◆ Encourage users to share their sustainable fashion stories using a branded hashtag.
- → Timeline and Milestones:
  - ◆ Campaign Duration: 3 months (September to November).
  - ◆ Milestone: Launch of the video series on October 1st.
  - ◆ Milestone: Publishing of an in-depth sustainable fashion guide on October 15th.

By creating a well-defined campaign strategy that takes into account your goals, target audience, messaging, content types, and distribution channels, you can ensure that your digital marketing efforts are coherent, impactful, and effective in achieving the desired outcomes.

Content Creation

Content creation is a critical aspect of your digital marketing campaign. Crafting compelling and relevant content that resonates with your target audience is key to capturing their attention and driving engagement.

Creating Compelling and Relevant Content:

1. **Understand Your Audience:**
   Continuously refer to your audience research to ensure your content addresses their needs, interests, and pain points. Personalization is key to capturing their attention.

2. **Align with Campaign Goals:**
   Every piece of content should serve a purpose aligned with your campaign objectives, whether it's educating, entertaining, or inspiring action.

3. **Value and Relevance:**
   Ensure that your content provides value to your audience. It should offer insights, solutions, or entertainment that genuinely resonates with them.

4. **Consistent Messaging:**
   Maintain consistent messaging across all content pieces to reinforce your brand's key messages and value proposition.

Tailoring Content to Specific Platforms:

1. **Social Media:**
   - → <u>Platform-Specific Content</u>: Understand the nuances of each platform (Facebook, Instagram, Twitter, LinkedIn) and create content that suits the platform's format and user behavior.
   - → <u>Visual Appeal</u>: Use eye-catching visuals, such as images, graphics, and videos, to stand out in users' feeds.
   - → <u>Short and Engaging:</u> Craft concise captions that capture attention and encourage users to take action.

2. **Display Network:**
   - → <u>Eye-Catching Imagery</u>: Create visually striking banner ads that convey your message quickly and effectively.
   - → <u>Clear Call to Action</u>: Use compelling CTAs that encourage users to click and learn more about your offering.
   - → <u>Message Simplification</u>: Due to limited space, distill your message to its core value.

3. **Digital Out of Home (DOOH):**
   - → <u>Impactful Visuals</u>: Use high-resolution images or simple animations to capture attention in a glance.
   - → <u>Short and Memorable</u>: Craft succinct messages that can be absorbed in a few seconds.
   - → <u>Location Awareness:</u> Tailor your content to the physical environment of the display location for enhanced relevance.

4. Connected TV (CTV):

→ <u>Engaging Videos</u>: Create well-produced videos that align with the longer-form content consumption typical of CTV platforms.

→ <u>Storytelling</u>: Use storytelling to create an emotional connection with viewers and effectively communicate your brand's story.

→ <u>CTA Integration</u>: Incorporate clear calls to action that drive viewers to take action, such as visiting your website.

5. Content Creation Plan:

→ <u>Diverse Content Formats</u>: Mix different content formats, such as videos, blog posts, infographics, and interactive content, to cater to various audience preferences.

→ <u>Content Calendar</u>: Plan your content in advance, considering posting frequency and timing to maintain a consistent online presence.

→ <u>Collaboration</u>: Involve a cross-functional team including writers, designers, videographers, and marketers to ensure high-quality content.

Example of Tailored Content:

→ **Platform**: Display Network (Website Banners)

→ **Ad Format**: Dynamic Banner Ad (300x250 pixels) with DCO

→ **Campaign Objective**: Increase website traffic and brand awareness for an online fitness apparel store.

→ **Target Audience**: Fitness enthusiasts, both male and female, aged 18-35.

→ **DCO**: Utilize dynamic creative optimization to personalize content based on user data such as demographics, location, and browsing behavior.
→ **Design Elements and Messaging**:
  ◆ <u>Dynamic Visuals</u>: Show fitness enthusiasts engaging in various activities, personalized based on user preferences.
  ◆ <u>Location Relevance</u>: Display images of local landmarks or gyms if user data indicates specific locations.
  ◆ <u>Demographic Customization</u>: Display workout apparel based on gender and age groups.
→ **CTA Integration:** The personalized CTA encourages users to click and explore products tailored to their preferences.
→ **Landing Page:** Clicking the ad leads to a personalized landing page featuring fitness apparel aligned with user preferences.
→ **DCO Benefits:** By leveraging DCO, the ad dynamically adapts to individual users, delivering content that resonates most with their interests, thus enhancing engagement and click-through rates.

By employing DCO in your Display Network banner ads, you can elevate personalization and relevance, delivering a highly tailored experience that increases user engagement and maximizes the impact of your campaign.

Set up Tracking and Analytics

Setting up tracking and analytics is crucial for measuring the effectiveness of your digital marketing campaign. By implementing tracking tools such as Google Analytics, Facebook Pixel, or other relevant tracking codes, you can gain valuable insights into the performance of your campaign, identify successful strategies, and make informed adjustments to optimize your efforts.

By setting up tracking and analytics, you transform your digital marketing campaign from a set of actions into a data-driven strategy. The insights gained enable you to refine your tactics, resonate better with your audience, and ultimately achieve your campaign objectives.

Importance of Tracking and Analytics:

1. **Data-Driven Decision-Making:**
   Tracking tools provide real-time data on user behavior, engagement, conversions, and more. This data allows you to make informed decisions based on actual user interactions.

2. **Measurement of Key Metrics:**
   You can measure key performance indicators (KPIs) such as click-through rates (CTR), conversion rates, bounce rates, and more to evaluate the success of your campaign strategies.

3. **Identifying High-Performing Strategies:**
   Tracking tools help you identify which channels, content types, and campaigns are delivering the best results, allowing you to allocate resources effectively.

4. **Optimizing Campaigns:**
    Continuous monitoring and analysis enable you to make necessary adjustments to underperforming elements, improving overall campaign performance.

5. **Understanding Audience Behavior:**
    Analytics provide insights into how users interact with your content, helping you understand their preferences, interests, and pain points.

Setting Up Tracking and Analytics:

1. **Google Analytics:**
    → Implement the Google Analytics tracking code on your website to track user behavior, traffic sources, conversions, and more.
    → Create goals to track specific actions users take on your site, such as form submissions or purchases.

2. **Facebook Pixel:**
    → Install the Facebook Pixel on your website to track user interactions, website visits, and conversions driven by Facebook ads.
    → Use the pixel to retarget users who have visited your site, showing them relevant ads on Facebook.

3. **Other Tracking Codes:**
    → Depending on the platforms you're using, implement relevant tracking codes like LinkedIn Insight Tag, Twitter Pixel, or Pinterest Tag, or third party pixels for DCO and DSP tools.

Examples of Tracking and Analytics Insights:

1. **Google Analytics Insights:**
   → <u>Traffic Sources</u>: Analyze which channels (organic search, social media, direct, referral) are driving the most traffic to your website.
   → <u>Bounce Rate</u>: Evaluate the percentage of users who navigate away from your site after viewing only one page.
   → <u>Conversion Funnel</u>: Track the steps users take before converting, identifying potential drop-off points.

2. **Facebook Pixel Insights:**
   → <u>Conversion Tracking</u>: Measure the number of users who completed desired actions, such as signing up or making a purchase.
   → <u>Audience Insights</u>: Gain insights into the demographics, interests, and behaviors of users who interact with your ads.

3. **LinkedIn Insight Tag Insights:**
   → <u>Audience Engagement</u>: Analyze how LinkedIn users engage with your content, such as clicking on ads or visiting your website.
   → <u>Job Function Analysis</u>: Understand the job functions of professionals interacting with your ads, helping you tailor content.

Optimizing Based on Insights:

1. **Iterative Adjustments:**
   Regularly review tracking data to identify trends and patterns. Make adjustments to your campaign strategies based on what's performing well or needing improvement.

2. **A/B Testing:**
   Use insights to conduct A/B tests, comparing different variations of your content, ads, or landing pages to determine what resonates best with your audience.

3. **Budget Reallocation:**
   Allocate budget to channels or campaigns that yield the best results, optimizing your resources for maximum impact.

4. **Content Optimization:**
   Adapt your content based on user behavior data, focusing on the type of content that engages users and drives conversions.

Create a Landing Page or Campaign Website

Creating a dedicated landing page or campaign website is essential for maximizing conversions and achieving the goals of your digital marketing campaign. These optimized pages provide a focused and compelling experience for your visitors, guiding them toward specific actions that align with your campaign objectives.

Creating a dedicated landing page or campaign website that adheres to these principles helps you guide visitors through a seamless journey, increasing the likelihood of conversion and achieving your campaign objectives. Regularly monitor the performance of your landing page using tracking tools to make necessary optimizations for improved results.

Importance of Landing Pages or Campaign Websites:

→ **Focused Message:** Dedicated pages allow you to deliver a clear and concise message tailored to your campaign's goals and target audience.

→ **Conversion Optimization:** By minimizing distractions and emphasizing relevant information, you create an environment conducive to driving user actions such as sign-ups, purchases, or downloads.

➜ **Relevance:** A well-designed landing page ensures that visitors find exactly what they're looking for, boosting their confidence in your offering.

➜ **Tracking and Analytics:** Dedicated pages make it easier to track user interactions, measure conversions, and gain insights into campaign performance.

Creating an Effective Landing Page or Campaign Website:

1. **Clear and Compelling Headline:**
   - ➜ Your headline should succinctly convey the primary benefit or value of your offer.
   - ➜ Use persuasive language that captures visitors' attention and encourages them to keep reading.

2. **Engaging Visuals:**
   - ➜ Use high-quality images, videos, or graphics that align with your campaign's theme.
   - ➜ Visuals should complement your message and evoke emotions related to your offer.

3. **Relevant and Concise Content:**
   - ➜ Craft concise, benefit-focused content that explains your offer's value proposition.
   - ➜ Use bullet points and subheadings to break up text and make it easily scannable.

4. **Strong Call to Action (CTA):**

→ Place a clear and prominent CTA that guides visitors toward the desired action (e.g., "Sign Up," "Shop Now").
→ Make the CTA button visually distinct with contrasting colors.

5. Minimal Distractions:

→ Remove unnecessary navigation menus or links that could divert visitors' attention away from the main action.

6. Social Proof and Trust Signals:

→ Include testimonials, reviews, trust badges, or certifications that build credibility and trust.

7. Responsive Design:

→ Ensure your landing page or website is optimized for various devices (desktop, mobile, tablet) to provide a seamless user experience.

8. Contact Information or Support:

→ Include a way for visitors to contact you if they have questions or concerns.
→ Provide clear contact details or a support form.

9. Thank You/Confirmation Page:

→ After visitors complete the desired action, redirect them to a thank you or confirmation page that reinforces their decision and provides next steps.

Example of a Landing Page for a Fitness Challenge Campaign:

→ **Headline**: Transform Your Body in 30 Days: Join the Ultimate Fitness Challenge!

→ **Visuals**: High-energy images of individuals working out, achieving their goals, and enjoying a healthy lifestyle.

→ **Content**: Briefly describe the fitness challenge, its benefits, and what participants can expect.

→ **CTA**: "Join Now" button that stands out, prompting users to sign up for the challenge.

→ **Social Proof**: Testimonials from previous challenge participants sharing their success stories.

→ **Trust Signals:** Mention partnership with well-known fitness trainers or nutrition experts.

→ **Responsive Design**: Ensure the page functions smoothly on all devices, providing a consistent experience.

→ **Contact Information**: Display a contact form for inquiries and customer support.

→ **Thank You Page**: Redirect to a page congratulating users for joining the challenge and providing details on how to get started.

Design Visual Assets

Designing visually appealing assets is a critical component of your digital marketing campaign. Eye-catching visuals, whether images, videos, or graphics, have the power to capture attention, convey messages, and evoke emotions. These assets, when aligned with your brand identity, enhance the overall effectiveness of your campaign.

Designing visual assets that resonate with your audience, align with your campaign message, and remain consistent with your brand identity enhances your campaign's impact. Regularly assess the performance of your visual content and iterate based on user engagement and feedback to continuously improve your campaign's effectiveness.

Importance of Visual Assets:

→ **Attention and Engagement**: Visually appealing content grabs users' attention and encourages them to engage with your campaign.

→ **Message Communication:** Visuals can effectively convey complex messages, values, and emotions that resonate with your target audience.

→ **Brand Recognition:** Consistent visuals build brand recognition and reinforce your brand's identity, making it more memorable.

→ **Storytelling: Visuals** can tell a story that goes beyond words, allowing you to connect with your audience on a deeper level.

→ **Emotional Connection:** Well-designed visuals evoke emotions that can influence user perceptions and decisions.

Designing Effective Visual Assets:

1. **Consistency with Brand Identity:**
   - → Ensure that your visual assets align with your brand's colors, fonts, logo, and overall design guidelines.
   - → Consistency reinforces brand recognition and maintains a cohesive look and feel.

2. **Clear and Relevant Imagery:**
   - → Choose images that are relevant to your campaign message and resonate with your target audience.
   - → High-resolution images contribute to a professional and visually pleasing presentation.

3. **Storytelling Through Images:**
   - → Use visuals to tell a narrative that connects with your audience's emotions and experiences.
   - → Show real people using your product or enjoying your services to make the experience relatable.

4. **Typography and Graphics:**
   - → Incorporate typography that complements your brand's voice and message.
   - → Use graphics, icons, and illustrations to visually communicate concepts, benefits, and data.

5. **Video Content:**
   - → Create engaging videos that showcase your products, explain complex ideas, or share customer testimonials.
   - → Keep videos concise and impactful to maintain viewer interest.

6. **Infographics:**
   - → Utilize infographics to present data, statistics, or step-by-step processes in a visually engaging format.
   - → Infographics simplify complex information and make it easier for users to understand.

7. **Emotional Appeal:**
   - → Choose visuals that evoke the emotions you want your audience to associate with your brand or campaign.
   - → Emotions like joy, inspiration, and empowerment can leave a lasting impact.

8. **Platform Optimization:**
   - → Format visuals to suit the specific requirements of each platform, whether it's social media, websites, or display ads.

Example of Visual Assets for a Sustainable Fashion Campaign:

- → **Images**: Showcasing models wearing eco-friendly clothing against natural backdrops, emphasizing sustainability and style.

→ **Videos**: A short video featuring the manufacturing process of sustainable fabrics, highlighting the brand's commitment to eco-consciousness.

→ **Infographics**: Presenting statistics about the environmental impact of fast fashion compared to sustainable alternatives in a visually appealing and easy-to-understand format.

→ **Typography and Graphics**: Using typography with natural elements like leaves and using icons to represent eco-friendly practices like recycling.

→ **Color Palette**: Utilizing earthy tones and nature-inspired colors that reflect the brand's commitment to sustainability.

→ **Emotional Connection**: Featuring images of happy and confident customers wearing the brand's sustainable products, connecting the audience with positive emotions and aspirations.

Schedule and Execute

Scheduling and executing your display advertising campaign is a pivotal step in ensuring that your content reaches your target audience at the right time and maximizes engagement. By strategically planning and scheduling the distribution of your content across various channels, you can maintain a consistent presence, optimize reach, and effectively communicate your campaign's message.

Importance of Scheduling and Execution:

1. **Consistency**: A well-defined schedule ensures that your audience receives content regularly, establishing a reliable connection with your brand.

2. **Optimal Timing**: Posting content when your target audience is most active increases the likelihood of engagement and interaction.

3. **Maximized Reach**: Timing your content distribution aligns with peak usage periods on different platforms, reaching a broader audience.

4. **Brand Recall**: Consistent posting helps reinforce your brand's message and identity, leading to better brand recall and recognition.

Scheduling and Execution Strategies:

1. **Platform Insights:**
   - → Utilize analytics tools provided by each platform to identify when your audience is most active.
   - → Review platform-specific insights to determine peak engagement times and days.

2. **Social Media Scheduling Tools:**
   - → Leverage tools like Hootsuite, Buffer, or Sprout Social to schedule posts in advance.
   - → These tools enable you to maintain a consistent posting schedule without manual intervention.

3. **Content Calendar:**
   - → Create a content calendar that outlines the dates and times for each piece of content to be published.
   - → Include different types of content, such as blog posts, videos, images, and promotions.

4. **Campaign Phases:**
   - → Divide your campaign into phases (launch, mid-campaign, conclusion) and allocate content accordingly.
   - → For instance, a teaser can be scheduled before the campaign launch to generate anticipation.

5. **Time Zones:**
   - → If your target audience spans different time zones, adjust your posting schedule to ensure content reaches each zone at an appropriate time.

6. **Ad Frequency:**
   → Manage the frequency of display ads to prevent overexposure, which can lead to ad fatigue and reduced engagement.

Scheduling and Execution for a Display Advertising Campaign:

→ **Campaign Objective:** Increase website traffic and brand awareness for a new line of eco-friendly home products.
→ **Campaign Duration**: 6 weeks
→ **Channels**: Display Network, Social Media (Facebook, Instagram), and Email Marketing

Content Calendar:

Week 1-2: Campaign Launch and Introduction (Monday - Sunday)

→ Display Network:
   ◆ Banner ads highlighting the new product line's features and benefits.
   ◆ Displayed on relevant websites and blogs related to sustainability and home improvement.
   ◆ Ads run from 9 AM to 6 PM, capturing daytime browsing hours.
→ Social Media (Facebook, Instagram):
   ◆ Teaser posts announcing the upcoming launch of eco-friendly home products.
   ◆ Posts at 10 AM and 2 PM, aligned with high social media activity.

→ Email Marketing:
  ◆ Send a campaign announcement email to your subscriber list.
  ◆ Schedule for early morning to be among the first messages recipients see.

Week 3-4: Product Showcase and Demonstrations (Monday - Sunday)

→ Display Network:
  ◆ Dynamic display ads showcasing different product variations based on user preferences.
  ◆ Ads displayed on lifestyle and home improvement websites.
  ◆ Run during lunchtime and evening hours for maximum visibility.
→ Social Media (Facebook, Instagram):
  ◆ Carousel posts featuring images of individual products with descriptions.
  ◆ Run carousel ads at 11 AM and 3 PM to target breaks and after-work browsing.
→ Email Marketing:
  ◆ Share user testimonials and reviews of the new products.
  ◆ Send emails in the afternoon to catch users during their downtime.

Week 5-6: Countdown to Limited-Time Offer (Monday - Sunday)

→ Display Network:
  ◆ Flash sale banner ads with a countdown clock indicating the end of the limited-time offer.
  ◆ Displayed on a wide range of websites with high traffic.

- ◆ Ads run throughout the day to create a sense of urgency.
- → Social Media (Facebook, Instagram):
    - ◆ Create video ads demonstrating the products in use.
    - ◆ Posts scheduled for 9 AM and 5 PM to capture morning and evening engagement.
- → Email Marketing:
    - ◆ Send a final reminder email about the ongoing flash sale.
    - ◆ Schedule for early morning to catch users' attention before the sale ends.

Benefits: By strategically scheduling and executing your display advertising campaign, you ensure that your content is delivered to your target audience at the most opportune times. This approach increases the visibility of your campaign, engages your audience effectively, and drives traffic to your website. Regularly monitor the performance of your display ads to make data-driven adjustments that optimize click-through rates and conversions.

Monitor and Optimize

Monitoring and optimizing your display advertising campaign is crucial for ensuring its success and making data-driven improvements. Regularly analyzing key performance metrics allows you to understand how your campaign is performing and make informed adjustments to achieve better results.

Importance of Monitoring and Optimization:

1. **Real-Time Insights**: Monitoring provides real-time insights into how users are interacting with your display ads, helping you identify what's working and what needs improvement.

2. **Performance Tracking**: Regularly tracking metrics such as click-through rates (CTR), conversions, impressions, and return on investment (ROI) helps you assess the overall effectiveness of your campaign.

3. **Continuous Improvement**: Optimization allows you to make data-driven adjustments, refining your campaign strategy for better engagement, conversions, and ROI.

4. **Adapting to Audience Behavior**: Analyzing user behavior helps you understand how your audience responds to different ad formats, messaging, and placements.

Monitoring and Optimization Strategies:

1. **Analytics Platforms:**
   - → Utilize analytics platforms such as Google Analytics and platform-specific tools to track the performance of your display ads.
   - → Regularly review metrics like CTR, conversion rates, impressions, and bounce rates.

2. **A/B Testing:**
   - → Experiment with different ad variations to see which ones perform better.
   - → Test elements like headlines, visuals, and calls to action to identify winning combinations.

3. **Ad Placements:**
   - → Analyze which placements (websites, apps, networks) are generating the most clicks and conversions.
   - → Adjust bids and budgets to prioritize high-performing placements.

4. **Audience Segmentation:**
   - → Segment your audience based on demographics, interests, and behaviors to understand which segments respond best to your ads.
   - → Tailor your ad content and targeting strategies accordingly.

5. **Conversion Tracking:**
   - → Implement conversion tracking to measure the actions users take after interacting with your ads (e.g., sign-ups, purchases).

→ Analyze which ads or placements are driving the highest-quality conversions.

Example of Monitoring and Optimization for Display Network Campaign:

→ **Metric**: Click-Through Rate (CTR)

→ **Initial Observation**: One display ad has a significantly lower CTR compared to other ads in the campaign.

→ **Optimization Strategy:**

- ◆ <u>A/B Test</u>: Create a new variation of the underperforming ad with a different headline and call to action.

- ◆ <u>Rotate Variation</u>s: Allocate equal impressions to both variations to compare their performance.

→ **Results**:

- ◆ New Variation CTR: 2.8%

- ◆ Original Variation CTR: 1.5%

→ **Action Taken**: The new ad variation's higher CTR indicates better engagement. Pause the original ad and allocate more budget to the successful variation.

→ **Metric**: Conversions and ROI

→ **Initial Observation**: Although one ad has a high CTR, it's not leading to significant conversions.

→ **Optimization Strategy**:

- ◆ <u>Conversion Analysis</u>: Analyze which ad placements are generating the most conversions and highest ROI.

- ◆ <u>Refine Targeting</u>: Focus budget on placements that are driving quality conversions.

→ **Results**:
- <u>Placement A</u>: 10 conversions, $1000 revenue, ROI 4:1
- <u>Placement B</u>: 15 conversions, $900 revenue, ROI 3:1

→ **Action Taken**: Allocate more budget to Placement A, as it has a higher ROI and generates quality conversions.

By consistently monitoring metrics and optimizing your display advertising campaign based on data-driven insights, you can fine-tune your strategies to maximize engagement, conversions, and overall campaign success. Regular evaluation and adjustments enable you to achieve your campaign objectives and make the most of your advertising budget.

Engage and Respond

Engaging with your audience and responding to their interactions is a critical aspect of creating a meaningful connection and fostering a positive relationship. Promptly addressing comments, messages, and feedback on your display ads can significantly contribute to the success of your campaign.

Importance of Engaging and Responding:

1. Building Rapport: Engaging with your audience shows that you value their opinions, leading to a stronger connection and brand loyalty.

2. Humanizing the Brand: Responding to comments and messages humanizes your brand, making it more relatable and approachable.

3. Positive Perception: Timely and helpful responses enhance the perception of your brand's customer service and professionalism.

4. Feedback Utilization: Engaging allows you to gather valuable feedback and insights that can be used to improve your products, services, and future campaigns.

Engagement and Response Strategies:

1. **Monitor Platforms:**
   - → Regularly check comments, messages, and mentions on platforms where your display ads are running.
   - → Set up notifications to ensure you're alerted promptly.

2. **Timely Responses:**
   - → Respond to comments and messages as quickly as possible, ideally within hours.
   - → Show that you value your audience's time and opinions.

3. **Positive Tone:**
   - → Respond with a friendly and positive tone, regardless of the nature of the comment or message.
   - → Address any concerns or issues professionally and empathetically.

4. **Personalization:**
   - → Personalize your responses by mentioning the user's name or referring to specific details in their comment.
   - → This shows genuine interest and engagement.

5. **Provide Value:**
   - → Offer helpful information, answer questions, and provide solutions to users' queries.
   - → Be a resource that adds value to their experience.

Example

Scenario: A user visits your campaign landing page for eco-friendly home products and leaves a comment inquiring about product availability and shipping options.

Engagement and Response:
User's Comment: "I love these eco-friendly products! Are they available for international shipping?"
Your Response: "Hello [User's Name], we're thrilled you're interested in our eco-friendly products! Yes, we offer international shipping to bring these products to eco-conscious customers like you all around the world. Feel free to explore our selection and make your eco-friendly choices. If you have any more questions, please don't hesitate to ask. We're here to help!"

Importance of the Response: By addressing the user's question about international shipping, you provide clarity and show that you're responsive to their needs. This interaction enhances the user's experience on your landing page and creates a positive impression of your brand's commitment to customer satisfaction.

Tracking and Engagement: Monitor the comments and inquiries on your landing page regularly. Keep an eye out for common questions or concerns that users are expressing. This feedback can guide your content updates, FAQs, or even inspire future campaigns.

Benefits of Engagement: Engaging with users who interact with your landing page fosters a sense of trust and approachability. By providing helpful answers and acknowledging their queries, you encourage users to explore your products further and take desired actions such as making a purchase or sharing their positive experiences with others.

Engagement on your landing page extends the reach of your campaign and helps create a community around your brand and products. Every interaction is an opportunity to build a positive relationship and turn curious visitors into loyal customers.

Evaluate and Learn

Evaluating and learning from your marketing campaign is a crucial step that helps you gather insights, refine your strategies, and continuously improve your future efforts. By analyzing the results against your initial goals, you can identify strengths and areas for improvement, ensuring that each new campaign becomes more effective than the last.

Importance of Evaluation and Learning:

1. **Data-Driven Insights**: Evaluation provides you with concrete data and insights on what worked and what didn't during the campaign.

2. **Optimization Opportunities**: Identifying successful strategies and areas of improvement helps you refine your tactics for future campaigns.

3. **Continuous Improvement**: Learning from past campaigns helps you build on your strengths and avoid repeating mistakes.

4. **Goal Alignment**: Evaluating against your initial goals keeps your campaigns aligned with your broader marketing objectives.

Evaluation and Learning Strategies:

1. **Metrics Assessment:**
   - → Compare actual metrics such as click-through rates (CTR), conversions, impressions, and return on investment (ROI) against the goals you set.

➜ Identify which metrics exceeded expectations and which fell short.

2. A/B Test Analysis:

➜ If you conducted A/B tests, analyze the results to determine which variations of ads, visuals, or messaging performed better.

➜ Use the insights to inform your creative choices in future campaigns.

3. Engagement Patterns:

➜ Study user engagement patterns to identify trends in ad interaction, such as certain times of day or specific ad placements that generated more engagement.

4. Audience Insights:

➜ Evaluate the demographics, interests, and behaviors of the audience that engaged most with your ads.

➜ Use this information to refine your audience targeting in future campaigns.

5. Feedback and Comments:

➜ Review comments and feedback from users who interacted with your ads. Identify common themes, questions, and concerns.

Example of Evaluation and Learning for Display Network Campaign:

Campaign Objective: Increase website traffic and conversions for a new line of outdoor adventure gear.

Goal: Achieve a click-through rate (CTR) of at least 2% and a conversion rate of 5% on the landing page.

Evaluation:
CTR Achieved: 2.5%
Conversion Rate: 4.2%
Impressions: Exceeded goal by 15%
ROI: Achieved 3.8:1, surpassing the target of 3:1

Insights and Learnings:
The CTR exceeded the target, indicating that the ad messaging and visuals were effective in capturing attention.
Conversion rate fell slightly short of the goal, suggesting potential areas for optimizing the landing page's user experience.
High impression count suggests that the ad placements resonated well with the target audience.

Actionable Steps for Future Campaigns:
Build upon successful ad elements and messaging that contributed to the higher CTR.
Focus on improving the landing page's user experience to enhance conversion rates.
Consider allocating more budget to ad placements that yielded higher impressions and engagement.

Benefits of Evaluation and Learning: By evaluating your display network campaign comprehensively and learning from its outcomes, you set the stage for continuous improvement. Each campaign becomes an opportunity to refine strategies, optimize tactics, and align your efforts with your business objectives. Over time, this iterative approach helps you create more effective, efficient, and impactful display network marketing campaigns.

Conclusions

In the dynamic realm of digital marketing, achieving success in display advertising is a multifaceted endeavor. It hinges on meticulously planned strategies, keen audience insights, captivating content creation, and astute data analysis.

To embark on this journey, begin by understanding your industry landscape and setting clear campaign objectives. Tailor your approach to resonate with your target audience, and select the most appropriate digital channels to amplify your message. Craft visually appealing content that aligns with your brand identity and utilizes the power of storytelling.

Implement tracking mechanisms to gauge campaign performance, and establish a dedicated landing page that guides users toward conversion. Maintain consistency in content distribution and cultivate engagement through responsive interactions.

As your campaign unfolds, continually monitor metrics and adapt strategies to optimize results. Upon culmination, critically evaluate achievements against your goals, learning from successes and areas that may require refinement.

By embracing this holistic approach, you will pave the way for a successful display advertising campaign that engages your audience, amplifies your brand, and drives measurable impact.

www.ingramcontent.com/pod-product-compliance
Lightning Source LLC
Chambersburg PA
CBHW071104260726
48661CB00006B/2447